THE GOLDEN AGE
OF TRAIN TRAVEL

Steve Barry

SHIRE PUBLICAT

Published in Great Britain in 2014 by
Shire Publications Ltd,
PO Box 883, Oxford, OX1 9PL, UK

PO Box 3985, New York, NY 10185-3985, USA

E-mail: shire@shirebooks.co.uk   www.shirebooks.co.uk

A CIP catalog record for this book is available from the
British Library.

Shire Library no. 778.   ISBN-13: 978 0 74781 324 8

Steve Barry has asserted his right under the Copyright,
Designs and Patents Act, 1988, to be identified as the
author of this book.

Designed by Tony Trucott Designs, Sussex, UK and typeset
in Perpetua and Gill Sans.

Printed in China through Worldprint Ltd.

14 15 16 17 18   10 9 8 7 6 5 4 3 2 1

COVER IMAGE
The classic lines of the luxury trains of the Atchison,
Topeka & Santa Fe Railway were the epitome of
streamlined passenger service. Featuring the most famous
paint design in US railroading, the Warbonnet, and a string
of stainless-steel cars, trains like the *Chief* and *Super Chief*
became icons of American transportation.

TITLE PAGE IMAGE
American tourists of 1910 taking scenic photographs from
the rear observation platform of a Union Pacific train.

CONTENTS PAGE IMAGE
The *Orange Blossom Special* on the Seaboard Railroad,
postcard of late 1940s.

ACKNOWLEDGEMENTS
First, thanks to my employer, Carstens Publications, for
use of its vast library of railroad materials. Once I delved
into the library, various works from two authors were
instrumental in much of the research—the late George
Drury, who was an incredible wealth of knowledge of
all things railroading, and Mike Schafer, the dean of US
passenger railroad historians. Thanks to my late father,
Ernest Barry, who got me interested in railroads at a young
age. And finally, thanks to all the rail historians who have
devoted hours and hours of time, often with little or no
return, simply to share their passion with others.

PHOTOGRAPH ACKNOWLEDGEMENTS
Steve Barry, pages 50, 52, 54, 55 (top and bottom), 56,
57, 58–9, 60, 61. All other images, including cover image,
Peter Newark's Pictures.

Shire Publications is supporting the Woodland Trust, the UK's leading woodland conservation charity, by funding the dedication of trees.

CONTENTS

THE RISE OF THE RAILROADS

THE MOST significant event in North American railroad history took place on May 10, 1869. On that date, the Union Pacific and Central Pacific Railroads met at Promontory Summit, Utah, for the driving of the golden spike and the completion of the transcontinental railroad. With just a few blows from a spike maul, east and west were united by twin ribbons of steel. It also marked the day the US railroads moved from adolescence to maturity—they had vanquished the stagecoach and the canal—ending a mere four decades of whirlwind change. The American Civil War was over, and the nation and its railroads were entering a new era.

The build-up to this golden age is a remarkable story itself. Railroads were well established in Europe by 1830, but were hardly present in the new world. Freight railroads began to appear, tied to specific industries such as mining, but passenger travel remained the domain of the stagecoach and horse. It wasn't until the Baltimore & Ohio Railroad (B&O) was chartered in 1827 that the idea of a network of rails began to take shape. The B&O instituted passenger service in 1831 to the suburbs of Baltimore–initially it was horse drawn, and later steam powered. Railroad mileage in the United States quickly boomed. In 1830 only the B&O's 23 miles was built. By 1840 the mileage had increased to almost 3,000 and by 1850 it tripled to over 9,000 miles. It tripled again by 1860, with over 30,000 miles of track constructed. Due to the Civil War, it would take twenty years for mileage to triple again, with over 92,000 miles built by 1880. Another 100,000 miles would be in use by 1900. Passenger-miles would increase along with the track mileage, surpassing 7 billion by 1865 and reaching 16 billion in 1900.

Early passenger coaches were not much more than horse carriages mounted on flanged wheels. It was the B&O's Ross Winans, one of the great innovators of early railroad design, who came up with the double-truck passenger car. Two sets of four wheels, one set under each end of the car, allowed for longer coaches and smoothed out the ride. By 1840 most railroads had adopted what is still the basic standard design for a rail car.

Opposite: Poster advertising Chicago & Alton Railroad, with route map ingeniously incorporated into reclining chair holding lady with fan, c. 1885. Pullman Palace buffet and sleeping cars were offered en route.

Golden Spike ceremony, May 10, 1869, joining the Union Pacific track with the Central Pacific line at Promontory, Utah, thus making transcontinental railroad travel across the US possible for the first time.

Other changes over the next twenty years included a clerestory roof that allowed additional light in the car and aided in circulating air. As railroad travel became more competitive, the cars became less utilitarian with each railroad embellishing its coaches to attract passengers. By 1855, railroads had reached the point where long-distance travel was possible, and to lure passengers the railroads started adding the first premium cars—diners, observation cars, lounges and more.

Early passenger trains featured no onboard amenities. At meal times trains stopped at stations equipped with dining halls, and passengers stayed in luxurious hotels overnight. Business travelers demanded faster service, though, and one way to achieve that was to keep the trains moving. Sleeping cars had been developed as early as 1830, but it was Theodore T. Woodruff who put the first fleet of cars in service in 1857. Unlike coaches, which were owned by each railroad, sleeping cars were operated by independent companies, as these cars might travel over several different railroads on each journey. Other sleeping-car companies soon entered the market, although most of these companies had a very short life when one dominant company entered the field. Dining cars entered regular service on the Philadelphia, Wilmington & Baltimore Railroad in 1862, although the food was prepared off the train.

When one thinks of rail travel, especially in the golden age, one does not think of pedestrian coaches, however. One thinks of the palatial first-class accommodations. To find the birth of those, one needs to go back to 1840 on the Camden & Amboy Railroad, when two coaches were equipped not with the standard wooden benches of the time, but with rocking chairs. Seat springs, upholstery and better protection from the outside elements (not only weather, but locomotive soot and sparks) all were part of the earliest first-class services.

That brings us up to that day at Promontory Summit in Utah in 1869. Rail travel was common from east coast cities to Chicago, albeit a bit rough. Most major waterways still had not been bridged, and track gauges still had

Directors of the Union Pacific (UP) in a luxurious private rail car during the construction of the railroad in 1868.

Poster advertising the grand opening of the Union Pacific Railroad route from Omaha to San Francisco "in less than four days, avoiding the dangers of the sea!"

not been standardized so a long trip still meant changing trains, sometimes involving an overnight stay at the connecting cities.

In the post-Civil War years, passenger car development was still continuing. From the beginning, cars were made from wood, but as the years progressed the materials got finer. Cherry and walnut became standard, although oak was used on some cheaper interior work. The first heated cars appeared around 1870, utilizing piping that brought in steam from the locomotives (and replacing the coal stoves which kept part of the car hot and left other parts cold). Air brakes became standard in the 1870s, dramatically improving safety. Vestibules at each end of the coach were initially open, exposing passengers to the weather and locomotive soot as they passed between cars; closed vestibules became standard by the 1880s.

Meanwhile, the fabric of the nation was changing as well. The mobility provided by the passenger train broke down regional barriers. Business could be more easily conducted between firms that were hundreds of miles apart. Railroad profits grew by leaps and bounds as passenger revenues outdistanced those of freight. And along with the fast passenger trains came a whole new category of business—express traffic. News could now spread faster as the magazines and newspapers of the time hitched a ride on the passenger trains.

The mobile nation was changing its lifestyle, especially among the rich. With a quick and luxurious way to travel great distances, Florida soon found itself as a vacation destination with the Atlantic Coast Line running dedicated seasonal trains. California also became a part of the seasonal boom, as the Atchison, Topeka & Santa Fe ran dedicated trains between Chicago and Los Angeles catering to the wealthy heading to the warmer climates for the winter.

The railroads were eager to cash in on the travels of the rich and famous, and marketing became a key strategy. "Name trains" came into vogue,

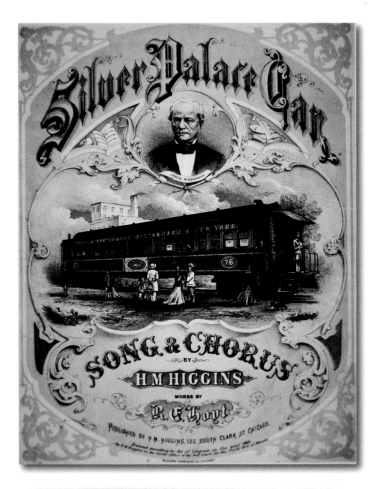

"Silver Palace Car" song sheet of 1868 in praise of the Woodruff Sleeping & Palace Car Company, running on the route from Chicago to New York.

Photograph of Midland drawing-room car, late nineteenth century.

Locomotive carrying officials on tour of inspection of the line, seated outside on pilot or "cattle catcher" of engine, for Chicago, Milwaukee & St. Paul Railway company, c. 1875.

Opposite: Colored engraving showing scenes from the inside of a sleeping car, c. 1880.

Advertisement for Palace Sleeping Carriage on the Rock Island route, 1878, showing luxurious interior and offering double sleeping berths for $5 between Chicago and New York.

including the Southern Pacific's *Sunset Express* in 1884, Union Pacific's *Overland Limited* and Atlantic Coast Line's *Florida Special* in 1888, and the famous *Empire State Express* of the New York Central in 1890. These trains had limited stops, with a desired average speed of around 40 mph for the length of the run. The Pennsylvania Railroad chopped seven hours off the typical running time between New York and Chicago with its *New York–Chicago Limited* in 1881.

One entrepreneur, Fred Harvey, realized there was money to be

Photograph of laughing woman traveling on the *California Limited* on the Santa Fe railroad in 1895.

made from catering to those who traveled by train. Working for the Chicago, Burlington & Quincy in 1872, Harvey purchased the Ellsworth Hotel in Ellsworth, Kansas, as a hotel and restaurant that serviced the passenger trains through town. Day trains would unload there for a quick meal before proceeding on, while long-distance trains would pause for the night. Harvey envisioned a chain of these facilities across the Burlington system, but the railroad wasn't interested. Harvey then took his plan to the Atchison, Topeka & Santa Fe, which agreed to a trial facility at Topeka, Kansas.

Engraving showing passengers being served food in a dining car, c. 1880.

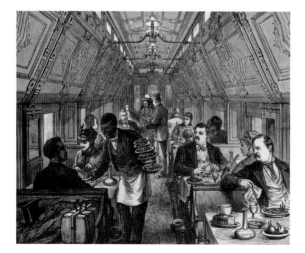

To say the Harvey idea was a success would be an understatement. By 1893 "Harvey Houses" were located all along the Santa Fe between Chicago and Los Angeles. Train crews would take food orders prior to arrival at a Harvey House, and the meal would be quickly and impeccably served upon arrival. The Harvey Girls, the waitresses at the facilities, became legendary as well.

Nonetheless, change was in the wind, and Harvey began transitioning from serving meals in restaurants to providing dining-car service to keep the trains moving. He expanded his reach by teaming up with the Santa Fe to provide luxury resort hotels, the most famous being the El Tovar at the Grand Canyon. The Harvey eating houses continued to provide meals into the twentieth century, eventually serving people who arrived by auto instead of train. Harvey dining-car service, the best ever provided, remained a part of Santa Fe's passenger service until Amtrak took over US passenger service in 1971.

The true golden age of rail travel was ushered in by one man and his company. George M. Pullman, along with Benjamin C. Field, rebuilt two coaches into sleeping cars for the Chicago & Alton Railroad in 1857. Other companies such as Woodruff, Wagner Palace Car Co., and Case Sleeping Car Co. were already established by this time, so Pullman was a latecomer to the game. But by 1863 he decided that he would make luxury cars his life's work, and that he would do it better than anyone else. In 1863, Field and Pullman ordered a palatial sleeping car from the Wason Car Co. that was more luxurious than anything else on the rails at that time. They built their own sleeping car in Chicago in 1865 that was even more luxurious, and it entered service on the Chicago & Alton Railroad; additional equally palatial cars were put into service soon thereafter.

Upon Benjamin Field's retirement, Pullman founded the Pullman Palace Car Co. in 1867, operating sleeping cars under contract for many railroads. He insisted on only the best for his customers; his cars became so synonymous with luxurious rail travel that the other sleeping-car companies soon were out of business. Pullman cars were operating over the Union Pacific and Central Pacific by 1868 (a year before the two railroads met at Promontory Summit). The last of his major competitors, the Wagner Palace Car Co., was absorbed into the Pullman company in 1899. By the turn of the century Pullman had a monopoly on premium passenger service.

Pullman developed the basic sleeping-car design that became the standard. Most of the cars in his fleet featured twelve "open sections" of

First luxury Pullman sleeping car, 1865. Color cutaway artwork published in 1938.

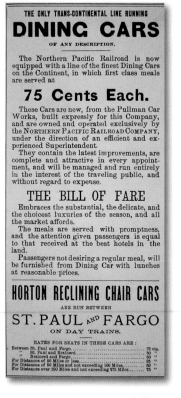

THE ONLY TRANS-CONTINENTAL LINE RUNNING

DINING CARS

OF ANY DESCRIPTION.

The Northern Pacific Railroad is now equipped with a line of the finest Dining Cars on the Continent, in which first class meals are served at

75 Cents Each.

These Cars are new, from the Pullman Car Works, built expressly for this Company, and are owned and operated exclusively by the NORTHERN PACIFIC RAILROAD COMPANY, under the direction of an efficient and experienced Superintendent.

They contain the latest improvements, are complete and attractive in every appointment, and will be managed and run entirely in the interest of the traveling public, and without regard to expense.

THE BILL OF FARE

Embraces the substantial, the delicate, and the choicest luxuries of the season, and all the market affords.

The meals are served with promptness, and the attention given passengers is equal to that received at the best hotels in the land.

Passengers not desiring a regular meal, will be furnished from Dining Car with lunches at reasonable prices.

HORTON RECLINING CHAIR CARS

ARE RUN BETWEEN

ST. PAUL AND FARGO

ON DAY TRAINS.

RATES FOR SEATS IN THESE CARS ARE :

Between St. Paul and Fargo	75 cts.
" St. Paul and Brainerd	50 "
" Brainerd and Fargo	50 "
For Distances of 50 Miles or less	25 "
For Distances of 50 Miles and not exceeding 100 Miles	50 "
For Distances over 100 Miles and not exceeding 275 Miles	75 "

upper and lower berths, for twenty-four beds in all. Each side of the car was lined with berths, and large curtains provided privacy. Each car had two washrooms, and most cars featured one or more private rooms at either end. "Hotel cars" featured kitchens for onboard food preparation. (Unlike sleeping-car service, dining cars remained under the auspicies of each individual railroad.) And the luxury wasn't just for overnight travelers. Even those only taking day trips could relax in Pullman style in cars featuring chandeliers and swiveling chairs. The upper class flocked to these cars, so much so that railroads operated entire trains made up of only Pullman cars.

By 1870 the railroads were the dominant force in the United States. Not only were they the top employer in the nation, but they were changing the man-made geography of the land. No longer was the worker tied to living within walking distance of his mill or office. If one could afford a commuter ticket, it was possible to move to the suburbs and enjoy a less crowded, higher-standard way of life. The alternate modes of transportation quickly vanished. Canals, which in the 1820s had risen to be the dominant freight mover, quickly died in less than half a century. Steamboat lines—which carried passengers along the navigable rivers of the country—quickly vanished, save

Advertisement for transcontinental Pullman dining cars on Northern Pacific Railroad in 1883, offering first-class meals served for 75 cents.

Photograph of the grand interior of a Pullman smoking car on the Southern Pacific Railroad, c. 1900.

for a few lines that simply carried passengers across waterways because rail bridges had yet to be built. The rail system had developed quickly, with many competing lines vying for passengers. This competition kept ticket prices low and trains running on frequent schedules. The business traveler, with many choices, found the railroads trying to outdo each other in offering luxurious amenities.

While the heart of the golden era is often thought of as the period between World War I and World War II, when the finest streamliners were running, the reality from a financial standpoint was the golden era was the final decade of the nineteenth century. Like the airlines of the late twentieth century, the railroads were setting themselves up for hardships rising from technological changes, financial turbulence and customer expectations.

Rare color photograph of a train pushing a snowplow, emerging from snow shed in Hagerman Pass, Colorado, 1899.

THE GOLDEN YEARS

BY THE DAWN of the twentieth century the competition among railroads was heating up. The single ribbon that had been united at Promontory Summit in 1869 was quickly joined by other transcontinental routes. Union Pacific, which had built westward to Promontory, split at Ogden, Utah, and through subsidiary railroads reached the Pacific at Portland, Oregon, and Los Angeles, California. Central Pacific, which had built eastward, became the Southern Pacific; in addition to meeting the Union Pacific at Ogden, it built its own transcontinental "Sunset Route" from Los Angeles to New Orleans, Louisiana, in 1881. It was joined in the American southwest by the Atchison, Topeka & Santa Fe, which built from Chicago to Los Angeles in 1887.

Meanwhile, the northern tier of US states was also getting a lot of interest from rail builders, first from the Northern Pacific, which completed its own transcontinental route in 1883. The Great Northern could operate trains to the Pacific as early as 1893, but it wasn't until Cascade Tunnel was completed in 1900 that travel was quick and convenient. The latecomer to the game in the north was the Chicago, Milwaukee, St. Paul & Pacific, which was finished in 1909.

All of these competing lines set the stage for a growth in the number of passenger trains in the new century. With most Pacific destinations reachable by multiple routes, railroads quickly realized they had to offer service that was distinguishable from the competition. The first twenty years of the twentieth century would see rapid change as railroads upgraded amenities, improved track and purchased larger and more powerful locomotives.

Due to the way the railroads developed in the US, there was no one "true" transcontinental railroad. Most trips involved changing trains in Chicago. But on either side of the Windy City, premium trains catered to the affluent. Probably the most famous was the *20th Century Limited*, operated by the New York Central (NYC) between Grand Central Terminal in New York and Chicago starting in 1902. The train developed from the railroad's efforts

Opposite:
Photograph of tourist sleeper car of the *Denver Limited* on Chicago, Burlington & Quincy Railroad, 1902.

Contemporary illustration showing bandits robbing wealthy passengers on the *Rocky Mountain Express* near Mudock, 1907.

to capture the crowds heading to the Columbian Exhibition in Chicago in 1893—NYC ordered a complete trainset from the Wagner Palace Car Company and the train operated on a remarkable twenty-hour schedule as the *Exhibition Flyer*. The train was so successful that a permanent deluxe train was established in 1897. Wagner produced another two trainsets of all luxury cars—sleepers, parlor car, club car, diner and observation car—which became the *Lakeshore Limited*. Still not satisfied, premium service (at an additional cost to the passenger) was raised to an even higher level when the *20th Century Limited* rolled its first miles on June 15, 1902. This new train ran on the tightest possible schedule and was given priority over every

other train on the railroad. But even with the additional premium fees being collected, the train ran on razor-thin profit margins.

The Central's prime competitor, the Pennsylvania Railroad (PRR or "Pennsy"), countered with the *Broadway Limited*, run between the same two cities. On the same day the *20th Century Limited* made its first run in 1902, the Pennsy countered with the *Twenty Hour Special*, timed to match its competitor.

Postcard showing a Santa Fe Railway passenger train speeding through Crozier Canyon, Arizona, 1910.

The *20th Century Limited*, New York Central & Hudson River Railroad. Postcard of 1920.

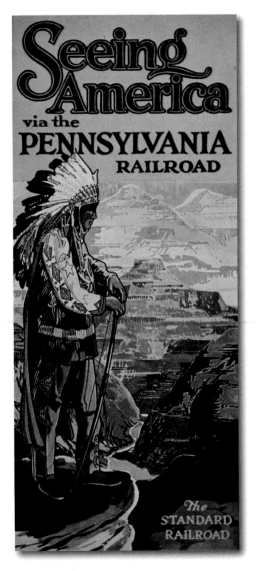

"Seeing America via the Pennsylvania Railroad," showing Indian chief looking at the Grand Canyon, publicity leaflet of 1928.

With both train names carrying a variation of the word "twenty," to avoid confusion the PRR train was renamed the *Pennsylvania Special* (which was still confusing, as there was already a *Pennsylvania Limited* in service between New York and Chicago). By 1905 the *Special* had cut the running time down to eighteen hours, and the Central was forced to match. The schedule was difficult to maintain, however, and the *Special* was rechristened the *Broad Way Limited* (named for the PRR's six-track-wide railroad between New York and Philadelphia, not the famous street in New York) on a slower schedule in 1912.

The *Broadway* (quickly renamed with one word) *Limited* was an equal for the *20th Century Limited*. It was an all-Pullman train and boasted the finest amenities. Unfortunately for Pennsylvania Railroad, it was the New York Central train that captured the public's attention. With its red carpet on the platform and celebrity passengers, the *20th Century Limited* was the glamor train. The *Broadway Limited*, though, found its niche as the train for powerful businessmen.

West of Chicago, the Northern Pacific operated the *North Coast Limited* between St. Paul and the Pacific starting in 1902. The Great Northern countered with the *Oriental Limited* in 1905. The truly great trains of the west, however, were still another three decades into the future, with one notable exception. The Atchison, Topeka & Santa Fe instituted a train in 1892 called the *California Limited*. The train carried one Fred Harvey-operated dining car to Kansas City, and stopped at Harvey Houses along the rest of its journey to the Pacific. It was discontinued in early 1896 but came back later that year as a seasonal bi-weekly premium train with all-Pullman service. It became a year-round train in 1900 and service increased to daily in 1905. But this train was just a precursor to a new service instituted in 1911. This new train, named the *De-Luxe*, was the most elegant service ever offered in the United States. The train had a six-car consist and carried only sixty passengers on each trip. It trimmed the running time for the journey across the west from seventy-two hours to a remarkable sixty-three hours. With an onboard barbershop and library, brass beds and an observation-parlor car, the train commanded a remarkable $25 surcharge over travel via more conventional trains over the same route. As the decades proceeded, the Santa Fe would remain at the forefront of premier passenger trains.

While the trains were grand, equally impressive were the gateways to the trains—the passenger stations, especially those in the major cities. The first two decades of the twentieth century saw the construction of some of the most magnificent stations ever built. Among the classics were Grand Central Terminal, built in 1913, and Pennsylvania Station, built in 1910, both in New York. These two stations were based on the Baths of Caracalla in Rome with high vaulted ceilings towering over an expansive concourse. Other cities would have stations of similar design,

The observation platform of the *De-Luxe* of the Santa Fe Railway, which entered service between Chicago and Los Angeles in 1911.

including Union Station in Washington, DC, in 1907, Michigan Central Station in Detroit in 1913, Kansas City Union Station in 1914 and Jacksonville Union Terminal in Florida in 1919.

Grand Central Terminal might well be the epitome of station design. With two levels of tracks underneath, it was and remains the largest railroad terminal in the world. And because of this design, it holds another distinction—as the first completely electrified station built. Since steam locomotives could not operate into the tunnels, electric locomotives were mandatory and the electricity used to power the trains also supplied the building. And with all of the trackage underground, Grand Central pioneered the selling of air rights above its property. In 1914, 470 trains used the terminal daily.

Perhaps no family is more associated with the golden age of railroad travel than the Vanderbilts, who were instrumental in both Grand Central Terminal and the *20th Century Limited*. At the time of the construction of the magnificent station in 1913, William Kissam Vanderbilt II was in charge of the New York Central, and the family legacy was well entrenched in railroading. Cornelius Vanderbilt took control of the New York & Harlem Railroad in 1865 and the New York Central in 1867. His son, William Kissam Vanderbilt, took control of the railroad empire in 1877 and relinquished control to his son and namesake in 1903. Upon the death of William Kissam Vanderbilt II in 1944, his brother Harold Stirling Vanderbilt

controlled the NYC until the family lost a proxy fight in 1970. Grand Central Terminal is full of the Vanderbilt influence, from its overall design by family architects Warren & Wetmore and Reed & Stem down to the acorns—representing the Vanderbilt family seal—which adorn everything from chandeliers to clocks.

Meanwhile, passenger-train equipment was undergoing a metamorphosis. As construction techniques improved and demand surged, car lengths increased to as much as 85 feet. The wooden cars of the nineteenth century, which were fragile and prone to catching fire in accidents, were rapidly being supplanted by cars of all-steel construction,

Photograph of passengers boarding the *De-Luxe* at La Grande Depot, Los Angeles, bound for Chicago in 1915.

Passengers boarding a Pullman car of the Chicago, Burlington & Quincy railroad in 1910.

bringing in the era of the "heavyweights." The first all-steel cars were introduced in 1907, and by 1910 they were in widespread use. Sleeping cars had become somewhat standardized in the 12-1 configuration, with twelve open sections and an enclosed drawing room. Pullman's fleet of sleeping cars included over four thousand 12-1s, about 40 percent of the total cars operated by the company. With the heavier cars came another development— the three-axle wheel assembly (truck). With a three-axle truck under each end of the coach, the weight was distributed over a wider area, and the ride was much smoother.

While this era seemed to be the best of times for passenger trains, at least on the surface, there were already hints that trouble was brewing. The years 1900–20 were marked by high inflation in the US economy, which occurred at a time when the railroads were making substantial capital improvements, especially in the conversion from wood to steel passenger cars. A huge workforce was required to operate the passenger trains, not only with on-train personnel but also several layers of management. The expectation of luxury and the demands of competition required that each premium train contain a lot of cars that didn't earn direct revenue—baggage cars, diners and the like—as well as low-capacity sleeping cars. Expenses soared and margins were thin. Throw in an unpredictable economy, and the problems were many.

Operating profits were beginning to suffer through all of this, although ridership growth masked the bad news. The Pennsylvania Railroad had made a half-cent in profit for each passenger mile in 1879. By 1914 that number had dropped to about a tenth of a cent. Gross revenues were rising, but a lot of that growth could be attributed to inflation. Meanwhile, the railroads weren't getting much help from the freight side of the ledger, as revenue per ton-mile was also declining. Politicians, concerned with getting re-elected, forced the railroads to maintain inexpensive fares on commuter routes, even if those fares only barely covered costs. Meanwhile, the commuter lines were getting competition from the electric trolley and interurban lines, which had substantially lower operating costs. And finally, the first storm clouds of what would ultimately doom many rural passenger trains were forming on the horizon—motor-vehicle registrations surpassed 5 million in 1917.

Still commuter operations were expanding as the big cities pushed outward. Philadelphia and Boston expanded their spheres of influence, while in the New York City area the railroads had made Long Island a convenient place to live while working in the city. Even in the midwest, where Chicago was growing in all directions, operations were expanding. On the surface, times were good. Just around the corner, though, was the biggest threat to passenger trains and yet another round of completely re-equipping the fleet to stay relevant.

Wealthy, fashionable passengers at ticket office of the Great Northern Railway at Chicago in 1920s.

THE *New* 20TH CENTURY LIMITED

NEW YORK - 16 hours - CHICAGO

NEW YORK CENTRAL SYSTEM

THE STREAMLINED ERA

THE HEAVYWEIGHT ERA, where passengers rode in six-axle cars built of steel, wound up to be short-lived. The railroad world was shaken up not by some innovation on the ground, but by the introduction of the DC-1 (and later DC-2 and DC-3) airliners from Douglas. Industry and design had come together, and the result was a sleek new look. With the airline industry embracing streamlining, suddenly the heavyweight steel cars on the railroads looked old fashioned. To help them compete, railcar builders turned to some of the best designers in the business.

Re-equipping the entire fleet was not something the railroads were ready to embrace. Passenger counts were continuing the steady decline that had started in the early 1920s, and heavy investments were still being made on the freight side to counter the growing number of trucks on the highways, all under the shadow of the Great Depression that had gripped the US. Still, most railroads thought they could still compete in the passenger market, and they put their best foot forward. Indeed, streamlining seemed to turn the tide. While passenger counts had slumped by a staggering 58 percent between 1921 and 1933, the numbers showed moderate increases through 1938 as streamlining took hold.

The Pullman Company, still the epitome of luxury rail travel, set the standard in 1933 at the Century of Progress Exhibition in Chicago. Named for the company's founder, the *George M. Pullman* served the role of the traditional sleeper-lounge-observation car. The similarities ended there, however. Gone was the traditional open observation platform that would bring up the rear of the train; instead, the car ended with a boat-tail observation end, punctuating a sleek aluminum body and rounded roof. Significantly, the car weighed about half as much as its contemporaries, and while no one knew it at the time, this silver carriage would foreshadow the streamliner era that was about to follow.

Streamlining was suddenly everywhere, from radios to kitchen clocks, under the direction of designers like Raymond Loewy, Otto Kuhler,

Opposite:
Poster advertising the *New 20th Century Limited*, sixteen hours from New York to Chicago. Poster by Leslie Ragan, 1938.

27

All-Pullman car luxury *Orange Blossom Special* on the Seaboard Air Line, heading for Florida sunshine in 1930.

Norman Bel Geddes and Henry Dreyfuss. The bright future that was portrayed by Art Deco design was the antithesis of the blues of the Depression. As applied to passenger trains, streamlining actually had little operational benefit. It was the marketing opportunities and the associated economic and aesthetic benefits that made the railroads convert.

The Baltimore & Ohio Railroad, facing stiff competition from the Pennsylvania Railroad in the market between Washington, DC, and New York City, began experimenting with streamlining and modernistic lightweight trains on its *Royal Blue* route. It ordered two eight-car trainsets for testing, financed partially by the Public Works Administration as a demonstration project. One set was made of Cor-Ten steel and would be steam powered; the other would be made of aluminum and diesel powered. The Cor-Ten set was delivered first and entered revenue service in 1935 after barnstorming the B&O system, although its first assignment was in service between Chicago and St. Louis. The aluminum set also entered service in 1935, and it operated on its intended *Royal Blue* routing. The lighter aluminum train did not provide a smooth ride, however, and it, too, was sent to the midwest.

Between 1934 and 1936 the streamliners started rolling on the railroads, mostly built as semi-fixed consists where the locomotive and cars were essentially one unit. Public response was overwhelming, and the new trains made the front page of the newspapers. The *Flying Yankee* entered service in New England on the Boston & Maine, while its cousins, the various *Zephyrs*,

headed out of the Windy City on the Chicago, Burlington & Quincy. Both of these featured a sleek shovel-nosed locomotive hauling an articulated set of semi-permanently coupled cars. Union Pacific started rolling streamliners to the west coast, while the Milwaukee Road did the same with its *Hiawatha* trains. Other than the Milwaukee trains, however, the consists may have

"Colorado Club" luxury lounge-observation car of Union Pacific's *Columbine* in 1930.

Afternoon tea
is served on the
Empire Builder of
the Great Northern
Railway in the 1930s.

been a touch too futuristic. The semi-fixed articulated nature of the trains meant it was difficult to swap out cars or extend consists—a mechanical problem in one coach could sideline an entire train, and potential passengers were turned away during peak travel times. The *Hiawatha*s were the first streamlined consist to be made up of separate cars.

The Pennsylvania Railroad turned to Raymond Loewy for its designs, including the redesigned flagship train the *Broadway Limited*. Loewy's most famous contribution to railroading, however, was his design of the sleek

Passengers listening
to radio in the
lounge car of the
Empire Builder in
the late 1930s.

City of Salina, the first streamliner diesel-electric express train, 1934.

but powerful GG1 electric locomotive that would power the Pennsy's passenger trains between Washington and New York. With a timeless styling, these graceful brutes would remain in service for half a century, not retiring until the 1980s. After designing the GG1, Loewy then turned his attention to steam, tackling the task of streamlining the railroad's ubiquitous Pacific-type locomotives for service on the *Broadway Limited*. In all, a dozen locomotives would receive the Loewy treatment. While most streamlined steam of the time was being designed with a slanted shovel-nose, Loewy broke with the tradition and designed his locomotives with a torpedo-styled front.

Meanwhile, the Pennsy's prime competitor, the New York Central, employed Henry Dreyfuss to redesign the *20th Century Limited*. With its sleek grey exterior punctuated by a boat-tail observation car, the train was

Below left: Art Deco interior of bar lounge on the *Broadway Limited* on the Pennsylvania Railroad. Design and drawing by Raymond F. Loewy, 1937.

Below right: Stylish streamline interior of observation car on the *Broadway Limited* on the Pennsylvania Railroad. Design and drawing by Raymond F. Loewy, 1937.

31

Modern interior of the bar lounge of the new *20th Century Limited*. Design by Henry Dreyfuss in 1939.

the epitome of class. Before dieselization firmly took over, Dreyfuss also designed some of the most elegant streamlined steam locomotives to power the train.

The Budd Company of Philadelphia became synonymous with streamlined passenger cars. It had developed the *Flying Yankee* and the *Zephyr* trains, and it perfected the Shotweld process that allowed the welding of stainless steel. Architect Paul Cret designed the cars to have unpainted silver exteriors with fluted siding, which became the standard look for streamlined cars for decades to come. Indeed, the last great streamlined train in North America, VIA Rail's *Canadian*, rolled into the twenty-first century with a consist of entirely stainless-steel Budd-built cars.

Pullman Standard, in addition to building luxury cars for the Pullman Company, was also producing coaches and other cars directly for the railroads. Eschewing Budd's fluted stainless look, Pullman Standard went for smooth sides with skirted underbellies painted in the colors of the owning railroad. Despite an offer from the Budd Company to share the Shotwelding technique, Pullman Standard decided to apply stainless sheathing over Cor-Ten Steel; the two metals proved to be incompatible, and the underlying steel eventually deteriorated, with the added problem of the stainless sheathing concealing much of the damage.

Perhaps the ones to feel the pinch of streamlining the most were the major steam locomotive builders. Nothing said "old" quite like the look of the traditional locomotive, and new companies were coming on the scene building new diesel-electrics that were easy to streamline. The American Locomotive Company (Alco) was the first to promote streamlined steam, advertising that it would design and build locomotives to customers' desires.

All-Pullman car *Merchants Limited* on New Haven Railroad between Boston and New York, shown here at speed south of Boston in 1937.

Most early streamlined steam was ill conceived, though, with badly designed shrouding trying to conceal the underlying technology. The famous designer Otto Kuhler noted in 1935, "Streamline freak locomotives have been built lately the world over. Most of them are badly conceived in their outline and their shrouding and covering; in most of them the inherent beauty and the 'personality' of the steam locomotive is lost." Kuhler also recognized that shrouding need not take into consideration actual aerodynamics, as the benefits were minimal. He instead urged that streamlining be first and foremost for aesthetics. Kuhler would go on to design streamlining for several railroads that were notable, as he heeded his own advice.

The first fully streamlined locomotive was unveiled in 1934 when the New York Central rolled out the *Commodore Vanderbilt*. A three-year-old Hudson-type locomotive was selected for the shrouding, and with its wedge nose it was certainly reminiscent of the Burlington's diesel-powered *Zephyr*s. Not everyone was impressed with the design, however, and some thought the locomotive looked more like an upside-down bathtub rolling down the tracks. Entering revenue service in 1935, the *Commodore Vanderbilt* would spend the next two years powering the *20th Century Limited*.

Meanwhile, Alco had built a pair of Kuhler-designed Atlantic locomotives for the Milwaukee Road's *Hiawatha*s in 1934. After testing and public displays, the duo entered service between Chicago and Minneapolis, completing the trip in a scheduled 390 minutes at an average speed of 63 mph. Since these locomotives entered life as streamliners (unlike the *Commodore Vanderbilt*, which had shrouding added), the sheet metal and supporting frame was integral to the design; still, underneath all the lightweight metal was a conventional locomotive.

Even though passenger numbers were eroding, the railroads made one last push at building grand stations. In 1930 Union Terminal opened in Cleveland with its Terminal Tower dominating the skyline, and Omaha's Union Station opened in 1931. Mission-Revival-style Los Angeles Union Passenger Terminal, opened in 1939, would be the last great passenger station built in the United States.

Other stations opened during this era, with some becoming enduring classics while others completely missed the mark. The New York Central opened its Buffalo station in 1930, but greatly miscalculated the size and location of the building. With its eighteen-story office tower, the station seemed out of place located away from downtown in a largely residential area. It never lived up to its potential. In Cincinnati, Union Terminal was constructed in 1933 with a supporting complex of express warehouses and locomotive-servicing facilities that stretched out for about a mile. Like the station in Buffalo, it never reached its full potential, save for the traffic surge of World War II.

One of the success stories, however, is 30th Street Station in Philadelphia, built by the Pennsylvania Railroad. Designed by the firm Graham, Anderson, Probst & White, this Neoclassical Revival gem is perhaps the most famous station outside New York City. Built as part of the project that saw the Pennsy stretch electrical wires from Washington to New York, it replaced Broad Street Station in 1933. After a steady decline from the time it was built, 30th Street has made a comeback in the twenty-first century as one of the busiest stations on Amtrak.

Fashionable ladies reading in rear lounge of the *Royal Blue* on the Baltimore & Ohio Railroad in 1936.

The success of 30th Street Station can be traced to its role in one of the largest projects ever undertaken to improve passenger service in the United States. Since the dawn of passenger trains, any passenger heading to New York City from the west had to change trains in New Jersey and finish the trip across New York Harbor by ferry boat. The lone exception was the Pennsylvania Railroad, which had tunneled under the Hudson River to serve the magnificent Pennsylvania Station in 1917. Still, steam-powered trains on the system had to change locomotives to an electric motor for the trip through the tunnel. Electrification was popular on some commuter lines around the major cities such as New York, Philadelphia and Chicago, but was not in widespread long-distance use. That changed in 1933 when the PRR extended its Philadelphia commuter electrification southward to Washington, DC, and northward to New York. Another extension westward to Harrisburg, Pennsylvania, was added in 1938. With high-speed electrification connecting the major mid-Atlantic cities—and the ability to go directly into New York without changing locomotives or boarding a ferry—the Pennsy was soon dominating the market, and 30th Street Station was right in the heart of the activity. While the *Broadway Limited* was cruising under the Hudson, the biggest competition—the *Royal Blue* of the Baltimore & Ohio—was still terminating in Jersey City, New Jersey.

New streamlined trains were spreading across the country. The Union Pacific launched a new fleet of trains coinciding with the introduction of diesel power. The M-10000, a fixed trainset, led the way in 1934. The UP's *Los Angeles Limited* was completely redesigned and relaunched in 1936 as the

City of Los Angeles, the longest streamlined train in the world, with eleven cars, trimming fourteen hours off the Chicago–Los Angeles running time. The *City of San Francisco*, running five times each month, soon followed, and was the most luxurious train on the railroad. The *City of Denver* was hailed as the world's fastest train for its average speed of over 75 mph on its run from Omaha, Nebraska, to Denver, Colorado. Meanwhile, in 1937 the

Southern Pacific used semi-streamlined steam power when it launched its famous *Daylight* trains that ran up and down the Pacific coast.

The rise from the ruins of the Great Depression made for grand times on the railroad. Just ahead, though, was the biggest challenge they would ever face, followed by a spectacular and swift decline. The streamliners would ultimately be not much more than a facelift on an aging industry.

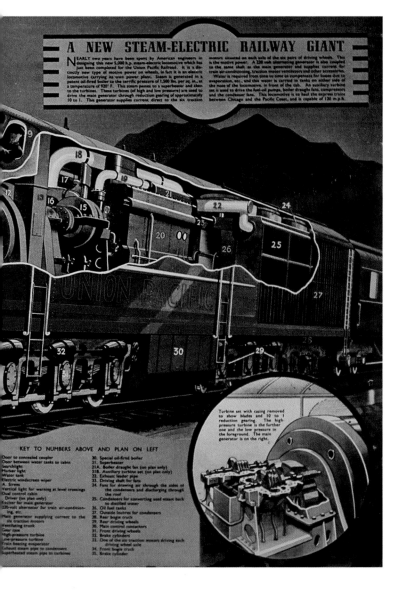

Contemporary cut-away artwork showing inside of Union Pacific steam-electric locomotive of 1939.

This Vacation Relax—

Go Pennsylvania!

All signs favor a vacation via a Pennsylvania train—for this way, *every* moment counts. Comfort and carefree relaxation are yours *all* the way! City lights . . . mountain air . . . sandy shores . . . whatever your vacation spot—your enjoyment will be greater because you get there refreshed.

Pennsylvania's streamlined fleets offer a wide variety of fine accommodations . . . overnight reclining seat coaches . . .

restful berths . . . all-private-room sleeping cars . . . *the choice is yours!* Pleasant Pullman lounge cars, beautiful dining cars, air-conditioning, fluorescent lighting, big picture windows, roominess and many more features. Let your travel agent plan your trip. Go by train *this* time and you'll go by train *next* time, too!

PENNSYLVANIA RAILROAD
Go by Train . . . Safety—with Speed and Comfort

A RAPID DESCENT

A T THE DAWN of World War II, passenger travel was already in decline in the United States. In the 1880s about 300 million passengers were handled by the nation's railroads each year, a number that grew to 600 million by the 1890s and had ballooned to over a billion annual passengers by 1920. The decline was steep, dropping by over half in the next decade as coach passengers streamed to the nation's highways in their automobiles. The streamliners of the 1930s stemmed the decline for a decade, and the railroads were about to get the last big bump in passenger traffic as the 1940s began.

With passenger counts declining, the railroads had already begun trimming surplus cars from their fleets. Suddenly, wartime restrictions on the use of automobiles sent people back to the stations, only to find that much of the shrinking capacity had been even further eroded by the diversion of equipment to move military personnel. Depots were crammed and chaotic, baggage was restricted and trains often ran with standing room only. Southern Pacific had eliminated twenty-seven daily trains in 1940 and 1941, only to find passenger counts surge by 374 percent in the first six months of 1942. Premium space in club and observation cars was being used for regular passengers, or the cars were simply dropped from consists and replaced by higher-capacity coaches.

To make sure military trains—which had priority over all other traffic—kept moving smoothly, civilian passenger trains were often delayed. To counter this, the railroads lengthened the schedules of many long-distance trains. Equipment that had been dedicated to one particular train was pooled to provide for more flexibility, and some car maintenance was done while trains were en route to reduce terminal dwell times and increase car utilization. The Office of Defense Transportation ultimately ordered that trains with ridership of less than 35 percent capacity be eliminated in 1945.

Everything changed in December 1945, just after the war came to an end. Suddenly, thousands and thousands of troops were looking to get home

Opposite:
"This Vacation Relax—Go Pennsylvania!" Advertisement for Pennsylvania Railroad, 1952.

Streamline 4-4-4-4 type Duplex locomotive class T-1 built by Baldwin for the Pennsylvania Railroad in the early 1940s.

in time for Christmas, with New York Central being forced at one point to stop selling tickets for eastbound trains from Chicago. But ultimately the end of war brought another decline in the number of passengers. Traffic had peaked at around 900 million passengers in 1944, and by 1950 ridership was down to about 400 million annual riders, about where it had been during the streamliner era of the 1930s.

Once the war was over, the last great re-equipping of passenger trains occurred. With factories and personnel freed up from the war effort,

Smart dining car of the new *Empire State Express* for the New York Central, 1941.

capacity was increased by locomotive and car builders as the railroads rebuilt from the rigors of the previous half-decade. At the top of the list was the changeover from steam power to diesel-electric locomotives—the writing was on the wall for the end of steam just as the war began, but builders had been prohibited from experimenting or expanding their product lines, as only tried and true designs were allowed by the government during the war. The upstart Electro-Motive Division (EMD) of General Motors began as a diesel-only builder, while the American Locomotive Company had started to augment its steam power with diesels prior to the war. The third large US builder, the Baldwin Locomotive Works, was entrenched in steam, and after the war it found itself well behind the other two in diesel development, a lag that would ultimately lead to its slow demise.

Coming out of the war, perhaps no railroad was as ready to embrace change as much as the Atchison, Topeka & Santa Fe. It had boosted passenger travel to a new level of luxury with the introduction of the *Super Chief* in

Painting of T-1 locomotive *Power for Pennsylvania Railroad Company's* calendar of 1945. Painted by Alexander Leydenfrost.

41

Rear view of the *Cincinnatian* deluxe passenger train on the Baltimore & Ohio Railroad, 1947.

Opposite: Lunch is served in an observation car on this advertisement for Pullman-Standard, the "world's largest builders of streamlined railroad cars," 1947.

1937. Its consist was a solid set of stainless-steel equipment from the Budd Company, punctuated by a boat-tail observation car. Adding to the train's striking look was a pair of streamlined diesels fresh from EMD; these slant-nosed locomotives were the first to wear what is largely considered the best railroad paint scheme ever devised, the famed Santa Fe warbonnet. Boasting a red hood that curved gracefully behind the cab windows, a silver carbody to match the coaches and yellow striping, the warbonnet quickly became the quintessential look of streamlining. The *Super Chief* would make its once-a-week journey between Los Angeles and Chicago in thirty-nine hours forty-five minutes; not coincidentally, this was the exact same time it would take Union Pacific's competing *City of Los Angeles* to make the same journey, a timing agreed upon by the two railroads. Though luxurious, the onboard amenities were not operated by Pullman; instead, the Santa Fe used the services of long-time partner Fred Harvey.

The Santa Fe's streamliners proved so successful that an additional sixteen Budd-built trainsets were put in service in 1940. A second complete *Super Chief* set was added, doubling the train's frequency to twice per week. Since the *Super Chief* was an all-luxury train, a companion all-coach train, the *El Capitan*, was put in service over the same route twice per week. One streamliner set was introduced as the *San Diegan* between Los Angeles and San Diego, while two more sets operated in Chicago–Kansas City service as the eastbound *Chicagoan* and westbound *Kansas Cityan*. Two more sets were put into service in California's Central Valley between Bakersfield and San Francisco as the *Golden Gate*, and Kansas City to Tulsa, Oklahoma, also got its own train as the *Tulsan*. Meanwhile, the *Chief*, an all-Pullman train that predated the *Super Chief*, also got a streamlined makeover. All the new trains were equipped with diesels from EMD except the *Chief*, which was powered by a streamlined steam locomotive.

At the end of World War II the Santa Fe turned its attention to improving onboard services. The *Chief* began to carry Pullman sleepers that were interchanged to the Pennsylvania Railroad's *Broadway Limited* and the New York Central's *20th Century Limited* in Chicago (also all-Pullman trains),

"TRAIN OF TOMORROW"—ON THE RAILS TODAY

General Motors **SELECTED**
Pullman-Standard

TO BUILD THE "TRAIN OF TOMORROW"

Observation Car..."Train of Tomorrow"

Teamwork between industrial leaders has turned a "dream" train into practical reality. It began in General Motors' Electro-Motive Division, with sketches of an idea to give passengers a "sky-view" room and other innovations for all-over travel enjoyment. They chose Pullman-Standard for cooperation—to develop designs based on safe, sound car-building principles; to work out complete, detailed engineering plans; to execute the idea and to build a train of Pullman-Standard quality. The result—an innovation in car architecture—is the product of this cooperation.

Whenever a new streamliner takes the rails you have growing evidence of the progressiveness of American railroads. The mark of quality on deluxe new cars is the Pullman-Standard nameplate.

© 1947 P.-S. C. M. CO.

allowing passengers a true transcontinental ride. With California now just one sleeping car away from the east coast, the Santa Fe embarked on a publicity campaign, rolling out Chico, the Little Indian Boy, who began appearing in all the national general-interest magazines such as *Life* and *Collier's*. The Santa Fe was not going to give in to the automobile without a fight.

Meanwhile, a couple of significant events were happening in the area of rolling stock. The Pullman Company had enjoyed a monopoly from the time it was founded by forcing railroads that wanted the company's onboard service to purchase its sleepers directly from Pullman. In a 1947 antitrust agreement, Pullman was forced to sell off its car-building operations, which became the separate Pullman Standard Company. The Budd Company and American Car & Foundry were immediate beneficiaries of the ruling, as the railroads could now

Advertisement for the *Chief* all-Pullman Streamliner service on the Santa Fe Railway, 1948.

Lounge car with Navajo décor on the *Super Chief* on the Santa Fe Railway, 1950s.

order sleeping cars from these two for use in Pullman-staffed trains.

Perhaps the most famous development in the passenger-car field in the 1940s, however, was the development of the dome car with its glass bubble protruding from the roofline. The idea for the car came from an executive from General Motors, C. R. Osborn, who was riding through the Rocky Mountains of Colorado in one of his company's new diesel locomotives and marveled at the forward view the crew had. He felt passengers should have the same view, and the dome car was born. The Chicago, Burlington & Quincy modified a standard flat-top coach in 1945 to create the first dome, and then General Motors and Pullman Standard teamed up to build and promote the four-car all-dome *Train of Tomorrow* in 1947. The first of the cruise trains, the *California Zephyr* between Chicago and Oakland, debuted in 1949, its schedule allowing for the best scenery along the route to be traversed in daylight. Because of tighter clearances on the eastern railroads, dome cars were largely confined to the western lines.

By 1950 most railroads saw that the age of the passenger train was drawing to a close. Costs needed to be cut, and that meant starting with the construction of new passenger equipment. Robert R. Young of the Chesapeake & Ohio started working with construction costs and car weights and determined the typical passenger car weighed in at 60 tons, or 1 ton per seat. Add in the weight of the locomotive to power the train, and the seat weight rose to a ton and a half. Car costs plus the allocated cost of a locomotive put the typical coach seat at a construction cost of $2,600. Diners and sleepers cost even more. Young argued that the cost of investment had to come down, as well as the cost of fuel and maintenance. The loss of passengers to the highways had made it extremely difficult for railroads to recapture their initial cost of investment on new equipment. The result of Young's vision was a lightweight train with a low center of gravity and

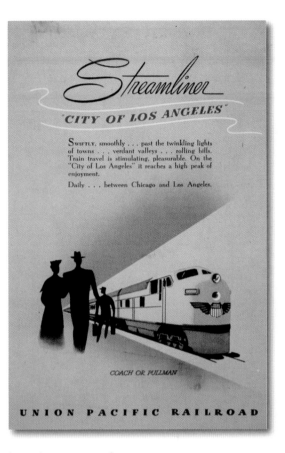

Stylish advertisement for Union Pacific Railroad Streamliner service between Chicago and Los Angeles, 1949.

"Smooth as silk," advertisement for Union Pacific Railroad's Streamliner service between Chicago and Los Angeles, 1948.

a futuristic look, which was dubbed *Train X*. Pullman-Standard built the first test train, which rolled out in 1951. It certainly caught the attention of the rail industry, and soon Budd and American Car & Foundry were building sets for other railroads largely based on the *Train X* design.

General Motors, which had participated in the *Train of Tomorrow* domeliner set, was eager to get into the lightweight train business, since successful passenger trains meant more locomotive orders for the diesel manufacturer. It borrowed heavily from the designs in its bus division, using components already in production, to produce the *Aerotrain*, perhaps the most futuristic train to come out of this era. Constructed as a semi-fixed consist, two ten-car *Aerotrains* were constructed for testing purposes. Each of the ten cars could carry forty passengers (much like the bus their design was based on), but the lightweight cars proved to be rough riding. Although the *Aerotrain* was designed for speeds of up to 100 mph, they were kept at conventional train speeds for passenger comfort.

Meanwhile, the branch lines were losing more and more money on passenger service. To combat the losses, the Budd Company designed a self-propelled coach called the Rail Diesel Car. Each RDC looked like a conventional coach from the outside, but under the car was a self-contained diesel engine and each vestibule was equipped with an operating cab, eliminating the need for a locomotive. The first RDC rolled out in 1949, and the cars were soon finding uses outside of branch-line service. Some railroads used the cars in commuter service, while others used them as inter-city expresses. Still, the RDC proved to only be a temporary fix for declining passenger revenues and many a branch had an RDC used on the last run over the line.

"It's Turkey Time," advertisement for dining cars on Union Pacific Railroad Streamliner service, 1950.

The mantra across passenger railroading in the late 1950s was "keep costs down." While lightweight trainsets were the rage, there was still a need for conventional coaches. The Budd Company was once again a leader in this area, as it developed a series of stainless-steel cars that were easy to maintain and inexpensive to purchase. Looking to lower the center of gravity on cars to help increase speeds, Budd developed the Keystone cars for the Pennsylvania Railroad. Low-slung, these cars had a depressed center area for coach seating, with slightly elevated lounges on either end riding over the trucks. The Pioneer III car was coach only, packing in eighty-eight people in its 85-foot length. And to meet the market of the economy sleeper, Budd developed the Slumbercoach, which could sleep forty people and would cost passengers only a bit more than a coach fare.

Advert celebrating fifty years of the *20th Century Limited* service between New York and Chicago, 1952.

The railroads had it pretty well figured out that by 1950, the typical rail-coach journey would be in the 200 to 500 mile range. Longer trips were still the domain of the sleeping car, while shorter trips were now being handled by automobile. Thus, the lightweight trains and high-capacity coaches of the time were geared to day trips. But in the late 1950s, the railroads would be hit from two sides by forces from which there would be no recovery. President Dwight Eisenhower

Dinner is served in a dining car of New York Central System, advertisement of 1952.

"Central" Attraction!

Mealtime magic no other travel can match

What roadside snack . . . what eat-at-your-seat tray . . . can compare to the fun of a meal on wheels in a streamlined New York Central diner?

Sparkling table. Attentive service. A varied and tempting menu. Every dish fresh from the stainless steel kitchen. Every course served with a big helping of scenery on the side!

Dining in comfort. Relaxing over refreshments in the lounge. Sleeping on the gentle Water Level Route. They're all part of your New York Central overnight vacation.

A vacation that gets you there *really* rested. And gets you there with *all-weather* certainty that no highway or skyway can match!

Like Breakfast in Bed? You can wake up to that comfort, too, on many a New York Central dreamliner. Enjoy it right in the privacy of your own hotel-room-on-wheels!

New York Central
The Water Level Route—You Can Sleep

championed the Interstate highway system, which made travel by auto over long distances much more palatable, and the airlines had developed the jet engine, making coast-to-coast travel economical and fast. Coach passengers streamed into their autos, while long-distance business travelers took to the skies. With soaring costs and a shrinking market, only government regulation kept passenger railroading going into the 1960s.

REMNANTS AND REBIRTH

A s the 1950s waned, the US railroads were faced with mounting monetary losses. Lower passenger counts meant the cost per passenger was rapidly climbing, yet the industry was heavily regulated by a government that would not allow fares to increase proportionately. Some railroads, such as the Southern Pacific, put no effort into maintaining its passenger service, and the trains soon became dank, dirty and seldom on time. Other railroads, notably the Santa Fe, took pride in its passenger trains, even if the trains lost money, and kept service at a high level. The jet plane had eaten into the luxury market to the point that few travelers demanded premium service; nothing signified the end of the era more than when the New York Central added coaches to the *20th Century Limited*, a train that had been all-premium Pullman service for its entire history.

The Pennsylvania Railroad found one venue where it could fight back against the airlines, and fight back it did, contracting with the Budd Company to build high-speed Metroliners. In a tubular shape not unlike the fuselage of an aircraft, these electric cars were self-propelled and designed for speed. Using Pennsy's electrified mainline between New York City and Washington, DC, the Metroliners would provide quicker downtown-to-downtown service for business travelers than the airline, since airports in both end cities were out in the suburbs. Alas, before the first Metroliner even turned a wheel, the Pennsylvania Railroad merged with its bitter rival, the New York Central, to create the ill-fated Penn Central in 1967. Not even the Metroliners could save Penn Central, though, and the company became the largest bankruptcy up to that time in US history when it collapsed in 1970.

Across the nation, though, the passenger-rail news was bad. While there had been 4,500 daily intercity trains in the US at the end of World War II, the number had declined to 600 by the late 1960s. Of that 600, the railroads had petitioned the Interstate Commerce Commission, who had the final say in such matters, to discontinue half of those. A consumer group, the National Association of Railroad Passengers, lobbied the US government to establish

Opposite:
Canadian Pacific Railway resurrected the luxury train on its lines in the early twenty-first century with the *Royal Canadian Pacific*. With a customer to staff ratio of almost one to one, it pampered guests while rolling through some of the most spectacular scenery in North America.

The major North American railroads such as Union Pacific keep the golden age alive with their business trains. These trains often run with diesel locomotives from the streamlined era of the 1950s and a matched passenger consist.

a federally supported rail system, which indeed came about in 1970. The National Railroad Passenger Corporation (NRPC) was created by the US Congress, with all its common stock owned by the country's taxpayers and all the preferred stock owned by member railroads. Any railroad wishing to shed itself from the liability of running passenger trains could join NRPC for a contribution of cash and equipment. When all was said and done, all but three railroads opted into the new system, which adopted the name Amtrak.

The original Amtrak route map was heavy on eastern railroads, while the western railroads wanted nothing to do with passenger trains, either operated by themselves or a government organization. The proposed route map showed only a skeleton service of mostly tri-weekly trains west of Chicago. By the time Amtrak's first day rolled around—May 1, 1971— proposed service had been expanded to more lines in the west with increased train frequencies. Amtrak was successful almost immediately in stemming the decline of rail ridership, as 23 percent more people rode trains in the company's first year than in the prior year.

While Amtrak was designed to operate on a shoestring budget, it did not mean there were no grand trains running in the US during the 1970s. Three railroads opted to stay out of Amtrak, with two of them operating a pair of the finest trains in the country. The Chicago, Rock Island & Pacific was one railroad that opted out; it operated a hardly luxurious service that wasn't much more than a couple of glorified commuter routes out of Chicago to the Illinois cities of Peoria and Rock Island. The Southern Railway, on the other hand, retained one train between New York and New Orleans, Louisiana. Operated as the *Southern Crescent*, the train featured mostly Budd-built coaches and sleepers behind immaculate streamlined diesels from General Motors. The Southern was always regarded as a classy railroad, and it kept its standards high.

The other railroad to opt out of Amtrak was the Denver & Rio Grande Western, which had operated a portion of the *California Zephyr* between Chicago and Oakland, California. The *Zephyr* departed the Windy City on the tracks of the Chicago, Burlington & Quincy, and gained Rio Grande rails at Denver. Once on the Rio Grande, it ran through the spectacular Rocky Mountains to Ogden, Utah, where it was handed off to the Western Pacific for the final leg into Oakland. The Rio Grande stayed out of Amtrak and retained its portion of the *California Zephyr*, operating it between Denver and Ogden as the *Rio Grande Zephyr*. Amtrak, which took over the *California Zephyr,* replaced the missing leg of the journey by rerouting its train over Union Pacific tracks through Wyoming, a far less scenic route.

Immediately, the *Rio Grande Zephyr* became the premier train in the United States. Like the *Southern Crescent*, it featured stainless-steel cars from Budd with the added amenity of dome cars to better see the scenery. And like the *Crescent*, it featured streamlined General Motors diesels for power. Alas, all good things must end, and all three hold-out railroads eventually joined Amtrak. The Rock Island's trains simply vanished when it joined in 1979, while the *Southern Crescent*'s route was added to the Amtrak map that same year. The *Rio Grande Zephyr*—now a passenger-train legend— would vanish when the Rio Grande joined Amtrak in 1983. Amtrak would reroute its own *California Zephyr* over Rio Grande trackage, giving up its bypass route through Wyoming.

From the time of its birth in 1971, Amtrak would spend the next four decades struggling for survival, even though its ridership numbers kept steadily increasing. Perpetually underfunded by the US government and never getting a long-term budget commitment, the carrier has scraped by year to year. Sometimes Amtrak's management was fresh and innovative, while other times it seemed management was part of the problem. A brief period of decentralization in the 1990s allowed regional managers to make localized decisions, and some trains began to stand out from the rest.

The rail-travel experience is more than just being on the train, and Amtrak has invested heavily in making its premier stations welcome gateways to its trains. The former Pennsylvania Railroad 30th Street Station in Philadelphia, built in 1933, remains one of the most impressive stations in the United States.

The *Coast Starlight*, operating between Seattle, Washington, and Los Angeles, was one of these trains; its regional manager found a way to improve dining services and other onboard amenities, including the introduction of the sightseeing lounge Pacific Parlor Car. Still, some years Amtrak was serving microwaved meals on plastic plates while other years you could get a meal prepared onboard and served on china. In the early twenty-first century service remained somewhere between the two extremes.

Like the Pennsylvania Railroad before it, however, Amtrak management realized in the 1990s that there were passengers to be found in the Northeast Corridor (which in Pennsy days was between New York and Washington, but now had expanded northward to Boston). It decided that it would go head-to-head with the airline business shuttles in the northeast and embarked on an ambitious upgrade program. Through the years, Amtrak had become owner not only of the former Pennsy electrified territory, but also the main line of the New York, New Haven & Hartford between New York and Boston. On the former New Haven, electrification extended only as far as the railroad's namesake town in Connecticut; Amtrak extended the wires from New Haven all the way to Boston. And to compete directly with the airlines in speed from downtown to downtown, it purchased brand-new high-speed trainsets that were named Acela. These trains were instant successes, and soon Amtrak controlled over half the market-share

of business travelers in the northeast. To make the entire experience more pleasant, Amtrak also refurbished most of the stations along the route, restoring more than a touch of grandeur to rail travel once again.

Even outside the Northeast Corridor, it seems America has not lost its love affair with rail travel. In fact, there is a very real resurgence. Amtrak's

Many cars from the streamlined era have been restored for railroad "land cruise" service. Among those is the "Babbling Brook," a luxury observation car built by the Budd Company in 1947. The car served on the New York Central's *New England States*, a Boston to Chicago streamliner.

Perhaps the most magical part of railroad travel is the dining-car experience. This setting is used on the luxury observation car "Babbling Brook."

55

One of the most successful luxury rail operations through the 1990s and into the twenty-first century is the *Rocky Mountaineer*. Originating in Vancouver, British Columbia, the train travels to Calgary and Jasper, Alberta.

cross-country trains, while somewhat utilitarian at times, often run at capacity. Only a lack of government commitment keeps the system from expanding either through new routes or increased service. While critics lament the government subsidies required to keep Amtrak running, they often overlook the fact that virtually no rail passenger service in the world—even the state-of-the-art high-speed trains of Europe and Asia—runs without government assistance of some sort.

More and more, though, there is a desire for a return to railroading's golden age, though not necessarily as a means to get from one place to another. In the 1980s a new phenomenon began edging across the US in the form of the dinner train. While the concept had been tried with varying success for many years, it was the Napa Valley Wine Train in California that established premium dinner-train service when it first ran in 1989. The railroad dining experience has always been a part of the lure of travel, and dinner trains have tapped into that lure. Many of these trains offer some of the finest meals available, all while offering the unique experience of scenery passing by the window during the meal. In the early twenty-first century the average number of dinner trains in yearly operation in the US is about seventy-five.

Taking the rail experience one step further, luxury trains have returned to the rails in various forms, offering not only the experience of the dining

car, but often the experience of palatial lounge cars and sleeping accommodations. Because of higher costs—moving trains over long distances requires not only fuel but usually a per-mile fee from the owning railroad—these trains have been only marginally successful. The longest lived was the *American Orient Express* which offered service throughout the United States between 1989 and 2008, sometimes as a stand-alone train and sometimes attached to a regular Amtrak train. The most successful in North America has been the *Rocky Mountaineer* in Canada, which began service in 1990. Operating through its spectacular namesake mountains, this train runs between Vancouver, British Columbia, and Edmonton and Jasper, Alberta. To maximize daytime scenery, nights are spent in hotels (and thus there are no sleeping cars) but otherwise the train is as fine as any that ran in the 1920s or 1930s.

Perhaps the final word on the golden age of rail travel should not be about what has vanished, but what has endured. And to find the last vestige from the golden age, we look north of the border to Canada. The history of the railroads of the northern neighbor mirrors those of the United States. Canada had its own golden spike ceremony in November 1885 when the dominion was united by rails at Craigellachie, British Columbia, and transcontinental passenger service started the following summer. Two railroads eventually spanned the country, the government-owned Canadian National and the

The "rail cruise" business has been difficult for many operators. The *Acadian* ran for only a couple of seasons in the early 2000s, traveling between St. John, New Brunswick, Canada across the border to Brownville Junction, Maine.

Previous page
The last great
streamliner in North
America is VIA Rail
Canada's *Canadian*.
Using stainless-
steel equipment
purchased from
Budd in 1950, the
train features up
to four dome cars
and an observation
car, and travels
between Toronto
and Vancouver three
times a week.

Opposite:
The *20th Century
Limited* boasted
the red carpet
treatment when it
operated for the
New York Central,
and passengers are
still welcomed in
the traditional way.

privately owned Canadian Pacific. Both vied for passenger traffic, but perhaps oddly it was the non-government Canadian Pacific that weathered the Great Depression and World War II in better shape. Emerging from the war, the railroad ordered 173 new stainless-steel passenger cars from the Budd Company, including domes and luxury observation lounges, and instituted a new train, the *Canadian,* on April 24, 1955.

Just as the passenger trains of the US were folded into Amtrak, the dominion's passenger trains were nationalized in 1976 under the banner of VIA Rail Canada. And like Amtrak, Canada's trains were vastly underfunded and eventually the rolling stock was showing significant wear and tear. But in 1988, when VIA embarked on a rebuilding of its tattered railcar fleet, it surprisingly put a large number of the Budd stainless cars through the program and restored the *Canadian* to its former glory.

As the twenty-first century unfolds, the golden age of rail travel may be decades in the past. But standing in the Rocky Mountains of Canada and watching twenty cars of 1950s stainless steel roll through the valleys, or riding in a classic Budd dome as peaks tower above the glass rooftop, one can still see that perhaps the golden age isn't really gone. It may not be as robust as it once was, and many travelers may not be aware that it is still out there. But with trains like the *Canadian* still crossing the continent and the fledgling rail-cruise industry still finding its way, perhaps we are simply in the spring of a new golden age.

The Pullman
Company operated
six barbershop/
lounge cars for the
Southern Pacific
in the glory days
of travel. One of
those cars, the 1949
"Overland Trail,"
is still in luxury
train service and
boasts an onboard
licensed barber.

PLACES TO VISIT

Railroad Museum of Pennsylvania, 300 Gap Road, Strasburg, PA 17579.
Tel: 717 687 8628. Website: www.rrmuseumpa.org
This collection includes several luxury passenger cars from the
nineteenth century, as well as steam, diesel and electric motive power.

California State Railroad Museum, 125 I Street, Sacramento, CA 95814.
Tel: 916 445 6645. Website: www.csrmf.org
A fine collection of western passenger cars and locomotives.

Steamtown National Historic Site, 150 South Washington Avenue, Scranton,
PA 18503-2018. Tel: 570 340 5200. Website: www.nps.gov/stea
One of the finest mainline steam rides in the US and a vast museum.

Illinois Railway Museum, 7000 Olson Road, Union, IL 60180.
Website: www.irm.org
A complete Budd-built *Zephyr* trainset operates at this museum.

The St. Louis Museum of Transportation, 3015 Barrett Station
Road, St. Louis, MO 63122. Tel: 314 965 6212.
Website: www.transportmuseumassociation.org
Among the pieces displayed here is a GM-built *Aerotrain*.

Colorado Railroad Museum, 17155 W. 44th Avenue, Golden, CO 80403. Tel:
303 279 4591. Website: www.coloradorailroadmuseum.org
Interpretative displays include the history of Budd's dome cars.

Pullman Historic District, Chicago, IL. Tel: 773 785 8901.
Website: www.pullmanil.org.
This restored industrial town was built for the workers of the Pullman
Palace Car Company in the 1880s.

La Posada, 303 E. 2nd Street, Winslow, AZ 86047. Tel: 928 289 4366.
Website: www.laposada.org
The last of the Fred Harvey hotels, built in 1929, immaculately restored.

Grand Canyon Railway, Williams, AZ. Website: www.thetrain.com
Luxury equipment in service includes a parlor car and classic dome cars.

Museum of the American Railroad, Frisco, TX.
Website: www.museumoftheamericanrailroad.org.
This collection includes motive power from the glory days of the Santa Fe.

Grand Central Terminal, 89 E. 42nd Street, New York, NY 10017.
Website: www.grandcentralterminal.com
Celebrating its one hundredth anniversary in 2013, this busy station has
been magnificently restored.

Mid-Continent Railway Museum, E8948 Museum Rd, North Freedom, WI
53951. Tel: 608 522 4261. Website: www.midcontinent.org.
This museum specializes in the restoration and display of wooden
passenger equipment of the very early twentieth century.

FURTHER READING

Barry, Steve. *Rail Power*. Voyageur Press, 2006.
An illustrated history of US motive power, both freight and passenger.
Barry, Steve. *Railroad Rolling Stock*. Voyageur Press, 2008.
An illustrated history of both freight and passenger railcars in the US.
Byron, Carl R. with Robert W. Rediske. *The Pioneer Zephyr: America's First Diesel-Electric Stainless Steel Streamliner*. Heimburger House Publishing Co., 2005.
Comprehensive history of the train that changed passenger travel forever.
Halberstadt, Hans and April. *The American Train Depot and Roundhouse*. Motorbooks International, 1995.
Coverage of railroad stations from small town structures to big city terminals.
Holland, Kevin J. *The Steam Liners: Streamlined Steam Locomotives and the Passenger Train*. TLC Publishing, Inc., 2002.
Detailed coverage of the good, bad and ugly in streamlined steam power.
Porterfield, James D. *From the Dining Car: The Recipes and Stories Behind Today's Greatest Rail Dining Experiences*. St. Martin's Press, 2004.
Recipes and stories from the dining cars of Amtrak, VIA Rail Canada and premier dinner trains.
Riley, C. J. *The Golden Age of the Passenger Train: From Steam to Diesel and Beyond*. Metrobooks, 1997.
A combination of railroad and passenger train history in both North America and Europe.
Savio, Tom and Anthony Lambert. *Extraordinary Railway Journeys*. New Holland Publishers, 2004.
A colorful look at the best train rides of the twenty-first century from around the world.
Schafer, Mike with Joe Welsh and Kevin Holland. *The American Passenger Train*. MBI Publishing Co., 2001.
Lavishly illustrated history of passenger trains and motive power.
Welsh, Joe. *Union Pacific Streamliners*. Voyageur Press, 2008.
A colorful history of the streamlined City fleet and its predecessors.
Welsh, Joe and Bill Howes. *Travel By Pullman: A Century of Service*. MBI Publishing Co., 2004.
Complete history of the service and employees of the Pullman Palace Car Co.
Yenne, Bill. *Santa Fe Chiefs*. MBI Publishing Co., 2005.
A history of the classic streamliners of the Atchison, Topeka & Santa Fe, including the operations of the Fred Harvey Company.

INDEX